Slippery Slopes

Slippery Slopes

A practical guide to happier skiing

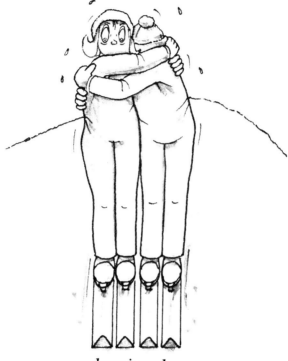

drawings by

Henry Brewis

and

words by

Harry Stone

Bridge Studios
Northumberland
1991

First published in Great Britain in 1991

by Bridge Studios,
 Kirklands,
 The Old Vicarage,
 Scremerston,
 Berwick upon Tweed,
 Northumberland.
 TD15 2RB

Tel. 0289 302658/330274

ISBN 1 872010 50 4

Typeset by EMS Phototypesetting, Berwick upon Tweed

Printed by Martin's of Berwick Ltd.

Introduction

It would be a pity to miss out on the sheer joy of skiing because you are under the impression that skiing is dangerous, that you are already a good skier or that you are too old to learn.

What has rendered such ideas not only obsolete but ridiculous is the highly scientific design of equipment today, and as long as you keep your speed in relation to your technique and are reasonably fit, you will be skiing for the rest of your life without disaster. (I have been skiing for thirty years without having suffered a break or even a sprain.) You can start when you are sixty and continue well into your seventies.

All right, you may think you are a really good skier but, even though you pass many on the slopes, try talking some lessons just to see if your assessment is right. Good technique adds considerably to your enjoyment.

This book is by no means a text book on skiing technique, rather it's a personal guide in the form of sensible and well-tested tips to accompany the drawings which illustrate the pitfalls, which are many and varied.

Etiquette

Pioneer skiers, up until the Second World War, were predominantly the upper middle class English and they observed conventional etiquette. Now, however, everybody can race down the slopes with more narcissism than any car driver but without rules of the road. Even in the tranquillity of virgin deep snow it is considered bad manners to allow your wedeling tracks to cross those of your companion. Good manners not only set an example, but contribute greatly to your safety.

Don't be shamed into carrying skis for helpless ladies
If they are strong enough to ski, they are strong enough to
carry their own

Don't be inveigled into standing farewell drinks to a ski class you've only just joined
Claim you are going up the lift for a final run down and will join them in the village later

Don't be mugged into paying for your ski instructor's lunch
He gets it free for bringing you there

Don't stop for a rest in a narrow section of the piste
You'll have people piling up on you.

Look right round before starting off
Or you'll have the equivalent of a car accident

Ski boots should not be worn indoors except in the hall and dining room
Worn elsewhere, you will tear holes in the carpets

Do not hide rubbish in the snow
Come the spring, it will remain hidden no more

14

Ski Technique

There is a world of difference between how good skiers appear to others and how they feel. Just look at all those people schussing in a self-conscious semi-cringe, perfectly convinced they are in a dashing racer's 'egg' position. So it is important to know how you should feel as well as look when you are skiing correctly. Also it is surprising how quite small points can make it so much easier to tackle such mundane irritants as sheet ice and narrow wood paths

15

Beware of crossing a deep snowtrack
You can easily come to grief

In smooth, crusty snow off piste watch for texture variations
Where the snow looks ruffled it will be soft for turning

Do not come to grief on sheet ice
Come to terms by sliding across, turning only on reaching the far side

Absorbing large icy bumps is exhausting on the thighs
Turn in the loose snow around the neck of the bump

Look for a lump or slight ridge when making a turn
It is easier when only the centre section of ski is in contact
with the snow

Put your weight on the outside ski
The grip is strongest on the inside edge of the lower ski

Learn and practice on dry ski slopes
Once on the mountain you can immediately take full
advantage of runs and lifts

Don't try getting up while your skis are still tangled
Organise your skis across the fall line below you so you first
gain a firm base

Instructors say 'put away zee chair'
They really mean bend at the ankles

Go to ski school
It's the best way to acquire real style

Try and follow the instructor's tracks exactly
It is good practice and helps those behind you

Controlled sideslipping adds the third dimension to skiing
Push against the slope below and you feel you are dancing
on air

Do not lose control on icy pistes
Turn on the loose snow on either side of the run

Looking up when you make a turn is not sufficient
Decide where you are going two turns ahead

To make a turn in broken or soggy snow, lift your skis clear
This means retract them under you like an aircraft
undercarriage

Imagine your weight forward on the tips when turning
Otherwise it will be like driving a car with rear wheel
steering

31

Slalom looks like a series of turns
But feels as if you are jumping literally from ski to ski in a
straight line

Lift Technology

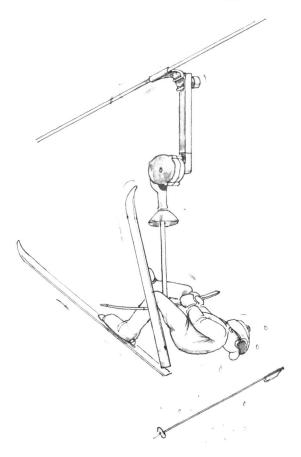

Skiing is a most unsatisfactory pastime. When you are at the top of the mountain you want to get to the bottom and when at the bottom you want to get to the top.

Today even moderate skiers can spend as much as a third of the day going up, so make a point of relaxing in the process and being as comfortable as possible.

Alone and lopsided on a T-bar can be tiring
To help counteract the tension, sit on your hand furthest
from the shaft

Don't get left behind in the lift queue
The strategic position is on the very outside line

The drag lift tows you while standing upright
Sit on it and you will collapse

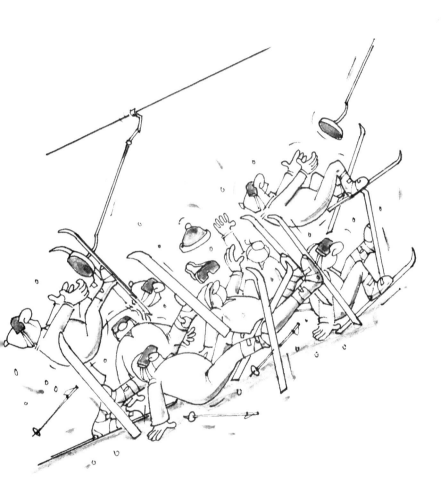

If you fall on a drag lift, get off the track quickly
Or you will wipe out all those behind you

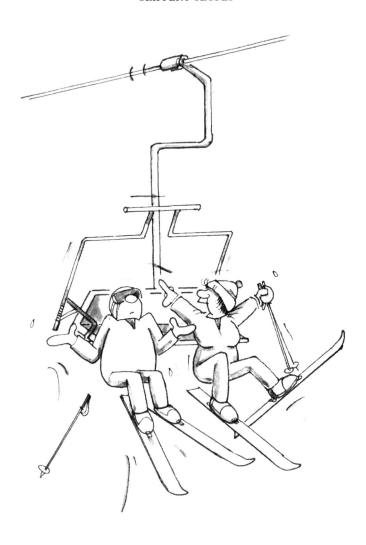

Keep your chairlift safety bar down as long as possible
If the lift stops suddenly your chair will swing into the
horizontal and will decant you

You can graft yourself on to a T-bar
Hold in front until you have gained sufficient momentum to tuck in behind you

Let the person furthest from the exit discard the T-bar
Or you will become entangled

Don't let anyone push you off the T-bar
Lean inwards from the waist, push on your outer ski and
it's the other person who falls off

Stop people overtaking you in the lift queue
Casually stick your pole in front of them between their skis

Avoid being lifted off your feet on a super strong T-bar
Take the bar from behind you and hold it in front until the
tension lessens

Equipment

Now that the performance of plastic at low temperatures is fully tabulated and the effect of friction on surfaces successfully computerised, season to season improvement in equipment is negligible. So, initially, hire – it's usually very good quality – and find out what suits you. Then buy the best – second-hand and at about a third of the cost.

Ensure your boots fit well at the ankle
They can be looser around your feet

On falling, you may not immediately realise you have lost your dark glasses
Buy a spectacle guard, on sale at opticians

Even well-ventilated goggles can mist up
A thin layer of moistened soap inside prevents this

Don't wear stoppers on your skis off piste
Fall in deep snow and you will have everyone held up
searching for your skis

Sharpening the ski edges is more reliable when done by hand
A machine is apt to do it only in patches

The ski stick baskets should be sufficiently open to see through
It makes it easier to thread one into another when preparing to walk

When off piste, have a long thong to anchor your skis to your boots
You will know where your ski is when it comes off in the deep snow

51

Buy boots only after first hiring them
Then you can be sure they really are comfortable

Safety

Being in good physical condition is one of the keys to keeping your skis elegantly together. It also means you are a much better skier and, above all, it means you are less likely to have an accident. Good physical condition does not mean a few hurried jerks two weeks before going out. It means working up to becoming properly fit over a period of several months. Try it. You will feel in good sorts even after the holiday is over.

Invest in an avalanche bleeper
A few pounds may well save your life

Beware of running out from shade into sunlight
Let your eyes become used to the change

If you feel tired, take the lift down instead of that last run
This is the time when most accidents happen

A succession of skiers means a ski class
Allow for tail-end-Charlie before carrying on yourself

Make sure insurance covers third parties
It can be costly colliding with another skier

If injured, do not declare you are insured until you get the bill
The doctor could help increase your future premiums by adding much more than 10 per cent

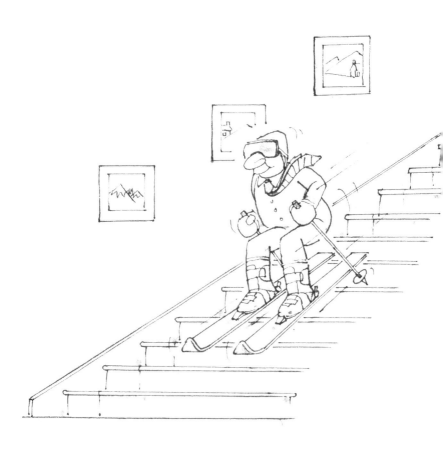

Start training three months beforehand
It will take a week to reach last year's standard

Do not over-exert yourself the first day or two
The thin air plays havoc with your heart

Try not to fall forward in deep snow
Slow compaction prevents release bindings from working

Do not let impatient ski instructors over-tighten your safety bindings
Loosen them again surreptitiously or ski very carefully

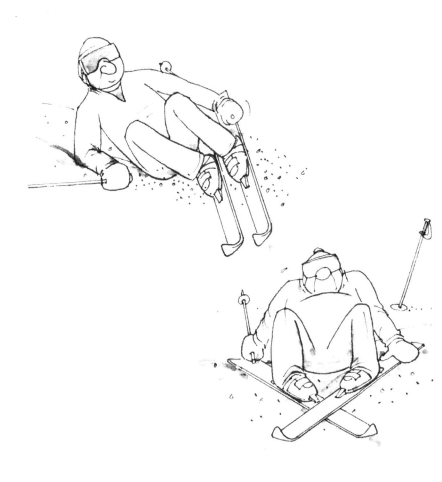

If possible, fall to one side of both skis
Fall between them and you are likely to tangle

Hold your sticks together between your legs and drag the points in narrow icy paths
It is bad form, but you keep control

File down the tips of your ski sticks
Or you may pierce your trousers – and your leg as well

Ensure Achtung *and* Attention *trip easily off the tongue*
They are the most effective words of warning

Avalanche coming your way and no escape
Take off your skis or crouch placing them firmly across the
fall line

Caught in an avalanche
Keep on the surface doing the breast stroke at least with
your arms

Give a stationary skier lots of room
Even ski instructors are known to start off without first looking round

Know how your safety bindings work
Otherwise your skis will keep flying off or else not come off
at all

Beware of convex slopes over 20°, especially if facing south
They are avalanche prone

Pairs of skis left outside shops are easily stolen
Place one around the corner so that it takes a thief time to
match them up

Tips in front please when carrying skis over your shoulder
When you turn round you may poke out someone's eye

Clothing

Do you prefer to ski or look smart? Magazines promote ski fashions and this year's colours. Designers refuse to provide adequate pockets as they spoil the line, and choose colours regardless of visibility in a white-out. Fur and woollen trimmings look attractive but they also attract snow which soon congeals into lumps of ice. Choose clothes for convenience and particularly for rapid fluctuations between heat and cold. Remember, a beautifully dressed bad skier looks ridiculous; with really stylish skiers no one notices what on earth they are wearing.

Wear several thin layers of clothing
It is warmer than a few thick layers

Do not wear ski socks outside your trousers
When returning indoors, coagulated snow melts into embarrassing pools around your feet

Buy a body belt
You can then carry cash and valuables with complete safety

Some salopettes are made of a smooth material
When you fall, you slide an awfully long way down the mountain

*Get a transparent envelope with tapes and wear your lift
pass on your sleeve
It cuts out endless fumbling in pockets at lift barriers*

Mits are much warmer than gloves
The things you can fix with glove-thick fingers are virtually
nil

Pertinent Points

In comparison with other holidaymakers, the skier is particularly prone to pitfalls. All that energy expended on the slopes – not to mention money – the cold atmosphere and the wetness of the snow. But there is also the uniqueness of the day, from the delights of black cherry jam for breakfast – and do remember to ask for it if it's not on the table – to learning the season's latest gesticular dance and wrestling the night away with too small a duvet.

Watching races on television, especially with a good commentary, is exciting
Standing beside the course watching one helmeted figure after another streak over a small section of slope is dull

With two stage cable cars, smart skiers get into the first cabin last
Then they are not left behind when changing into the second and usually smaller cabin

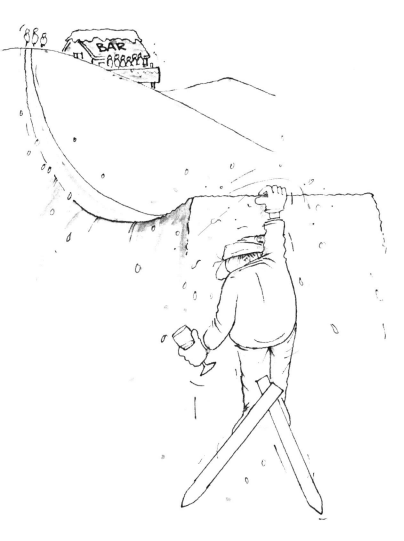

Alcohol imparts bravado
It also reduces the sense of balance

Avoid sore throats at nights
Dampen the atmosphere by filling your washbasin before
going to bed

Take a photograph out with you suitable for your lift pass
It saves time and inconvenience

If possible, ski in March
Daylight is two hours longer than in January

Choose a resort in a valley running east-west
The sun has the full length of the valley to shine along when it is low

Elastoplast is excellent over chaffing skin
It sticks with the skin rather than the frictional surface